BASEBALL IN
SOUTH BEND

Stanley Coveleski chose South Bend as his home after retiring from Major League Baseball in 1928. Support by his adopted hometown led to his election to the baseball Hall of Fame in 1969. In 1987, the City of South Bend dedicated their new minor league stadium to his memory. Today, Stanley Coveleski Regional Stadium is home to the Single-A Midwest League South Bend SilverHawks as well as a variety of local amateur baseball teams.

BASEBALL IN SOUTH BEND

John M. Kovach

ARCADIA

Published by Arcadia Publishing
Charleston SC, Chicago IL, Portsmouth NH, San Francisco CA

Printed in Great Britain

Library of Congress Catalog Card Number: 20040944

For all general information contact Arcadia Publishing at:
Telephone 843-853-2070
Fax 843-853-0044
E-mail sales@arcadiapublishing.com
For customer service and orders:
Toll-Free 1-888-313-2665

Visit us on the internet at http://www.arcadiapublishing.com

CONTENTS

ACKNOWLEDGMENTS

First and foremost, I want to thank my wife Lisa and daughters Emily, Irina and Marina for always being understanding whenever dad is doing something with baseball, on or off the field, and being the first to listen to the newest (or sometimes the oldest) baseball stories!

Next, I want to thank Dave Bainbridge from the Northern Indiana Center for History who let me work with him in 1985 on an exhibit on the early years of South Bend baseball history. A special thanks goes to the former and current staff members of the St. Joseph County Public Library Local History & Genealogy Room: Mary Waterson, John Palmer, Jane Spencer, Helena Hayes and Franklin Sheneman for their help, ideas and willingness to accept the fact that baseball can be worked into virtually any conversation!

And a thanks for the support of all my colleagues, co-workers and students at the Cushwa-Leighton Library at Saint Mary's College.

To the individuals photographed or who provided the opportunity to use some wonderful images: Carrie Pappa's wonderful shots of the South Bend Blue Sox the past two years; D. Brent Miller, for his great shots of the South Bend SilverHawks; the Northern Indian Center for History; and the Studebaker National Museum.

Thanks as well go out to all individuals and organizations who provided additional images without wishing to be named.

Finally, a special thank you to my editor, Jeff Ruetsche, and the Arcadia Publishing staff for their patience and willingness to give me "just two more weeks" . . . at least three different times!

INTRODUCTION

Baseball can be viewed in so many different ways. To some, it is a slow game; to others, it is timeless. In a way, they are both correct. How many times do people argue about who is the best at a particular position? How many times is there a definitive answer? What do you use as criteria—players from the same era or players who played 50 years apart?

No other sport invokes such feelings or passion whether you are talking about its current players or those from a century ago. In the sociologists world, baseball can be shown as one of the tools used by immigrants to become part of the "great melting pot." This can be seen in the last names of those who are playing the game and how each ethnic group gains acceptance when their names become commonplace on the ball diamond.

Much of the same can be said for the game in South Bend. Not only did the children of immigrants get to become more "American" by playing baseball, their own ethnic groups were fiercely proud of their accomplishments.

Sadly though, for every photograph or story that is in this book, easily there are 10 that have not been documented or, if the information exists, it is hidden away. Hopefully, looking through this book might help uncover much more about the rich baseball heritage that is a part of South Bend.

Known as the "Father of South Bend Baseball," Henry Benjamin spent less than five years in the city, yet his love and interest of the game of baseball is still being enjoyed in the community over 140 years later.

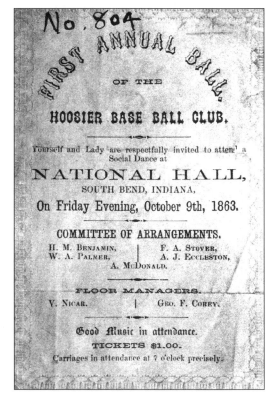

No. 804

FIRST ANNUAL BALL

OF THE

HOOSIER BASE BALL CLUB.

Yourself and Lady are respectfully invited to atten' a Social Dance at

NATIONAL HALL,

SOUTH BEND, INDIANA,

On Friday Evening, October 9th, 1863.

COMMITTEE OF ARRANGEMENTS.

H. M. BENJAMIN,   F. A. STOVER,
W. A. PALMER,   A. J. ECCLESTON,
          A. McDONALD.

FLOOR MANAGERS.

V. NICAR.   GEO. F. CORBY.

Good Music in attendance.

TICKETS $1.00.

Carriages in attendance at 7 o'clock precisely.

This is one of the few items in existence that shows the involvement by Henry Benjamin and early South Bend baseball. This is a program for a fund raising ball. As is the case with many amateur teams today, the ball was a way to cover expenses of their team.

ONE

First Inning

Roots of the Game

When you think of a pioneer, you think of an individual whose name is forever part of whatever history with which it is associated. However, Henry Benjamin, who is given the credit of introducing the sport of baseball to South Bend in 1860, is truly a mysterious individual.

Most of what we know about him personally comes from the reflections of people who knew of him at that time. A series of interviews with a number of the early players in South Bend was written in 1932. Most of their information places Benjamin in South Bend from late 1859 to late 1863. He does not show up in the 1860 census in South Bend and is gone before 1870.

Benjamin is said to have come to South Bend from the East and he operated a clothing store in the downtown business district. It was at this store that he met Walter Munson who was interested in Benjamin's stories about the game of baseball.

Their enthusiasm sparked more local interest and in the spring, the South Bend Base Ball Club was organized. On a given day, according to the stories, those who were interested in playing would come to a selected location and side would be chosen.

Even during the period of the Civil War, baseball events would take place. The local club at this time was often referred to by their new nickname, the "Hoosier Base Ball Club."

By 1863, the local game had attracted so much interest that the "Hoosiers" had competition from two other local teams, the Excelsiors and Rough-and-Readys.

However, following your favorite local team would become difficult between late 1863 and 1865 with the Civil War still raging—no newspaper was published during that time in South Bend.

By 1866, things began to return to normal as far as the local baseball clubs were concerned. In October of that year, the Excelsiors sponsored the first baseball tournament in the state of Indiana. Twelve teams were entered and a team from LaPorte, Indiana, defeated a club from Niles, Michigan, by a score of 31 to 29. The Rough-and-Readys won first place in the junior club bracket (a junior club was one that did not have state or national affiliations). The prize won by the Rough-and-Readys was $50 and the game ball. That ball is now in the permanent collection at the Northern Indiana Center For History in South Bend.

More and more teams began to play baseball in South Bend, and by 1870 there were no less than ten different teams! One of those teams was set to dominate local baseball for the next seven years. The Clippers were organized in 1870. They became the first team from South Bend to travel extensively. During their first season, they traveled to the Indiana cities of Fort

Wayne, Goshen, Elkhart and LaPorte. They also played against teams from Niles and Buchanan, Michigan. That same season, the Clippers became the first local team to wear uniforms during their games.

A number of local baseball "firsts" would be entered into the books by the Clippers. On July 30, 1874, the Clippers hosted the first professional team to play in South Bend. The Brooklyn Atlantics of the National Association drew a record crowd at the old fairgrounds (many of whom paid up to 25¢ for admission). The Atlantics won handily that day by a score of 32 to 6.

Just a few days before that game, the Clippers won the right to play the Atlantics by defeating the "Red Neck Nine" team from the University of Notre Dame. The victory over the Red Neck Nine was for the baseball championship of St. Joseph County. The game, which went 11 innings, was the first extra inning game played by a South Bend team.

The last major "first" by the Clippers was a shutout of an opponent. On June 11, 1875, the Clippers defeated the Snatchers by a score of 13 to 0.

Although the Clippers established many firsts during their playing days, it was nearly time for their sails to fold, as a new ballclub was about to come on to the horizon.

Henry Benjamin found a kindred spirit in South Bend when he met Walter Munson. It was Munson who shared an interest in the game of baseball, something few of the local citizens would know about. Munson helped Benjamin with the organizing of the South Bend Base Ball Club in the spring of 1860.

Baseball would not be the same game without an umpire. Even in its earliest days, the umpire made sure all the rules were followed. South Bend was no different as its first arbitrator was Dr. Robert Harris. During the early days with just the South Bend Base Ball Club playing, Harris would wear two hats: one of an umpire and the other of a scorekeeper. He later took to the field as a player with the Excelsior team.

This collection of early South Bend Baseball players had their impact on the local game seen for nearly 30 years. Pictured from left to right are Horace Van Tuyl, Jefferson Thompson, G.C. Rose, H.S. Stanfield, Judge Hagerty, Dennis Brownfield, Alex Staples, John Dunn and Charles Heaton. Van Tuyl, Dunn and Thompson all played with both the South Bend Baseball Club and later the Hoosiers. Dunn, Stanfield and Hagerty each had playing time with the Excelsiors. Finally, Stanfield and Staples would continue their association and involvement with the sport of baseball into the mid-to-late 1870s. They played a key role in the organization and success of the South Bend Greenstockings. Stanfield and his brother, E.P., helped that team secure the land for their ballpark, which would become the first enclosed baseball park in northern Indiana. Staples was involved with the building of that first park. A house and building mover by trade, he drove the posts into the ground for that first showcase facility of South Bend baseball.

These were the members of the Excelsiors Base Ball Club in South Bend. This photograph, taken in the late 1860s, shows from left to right, D. Holland, O.H. Palmer, L. Staples, J. Hagerty, H.S. Stanfield, J. Fisher, J.P. Creed, R. Harris, J.W. Camper, E. Nicar, W.P. Aylesworth, C.B. Stephenson, R. J. Chestnutwood, J. H. Dunn, T. Taylor, T. Witherill, B.F.

Dunn and G. Ford. Whenever the Excelsiors battled the local Rough-and-Readys, a virtual civic holiday was declared and nearly the entire city would turn out for those games that were played at Taylor's Field.

Base Ball Match.

As mentioned last week a match game of Base Ball was played on the 20th inst., at Laporte between the Laporte Club and the Excelsior Club of South Bend. The day was windy and unfavorable, but a large crowd was present. Everything passed of pleasantly, as the members of both clubs are gentlemen. The plying began at half-past one and lasted three hours. The result as given below, was furnished us by Mr. Stanfield of the Excelsior Club. Another game is to be played soon between the two clubs, and at this place:

BATTING.

EXCELSIOR.	O.	R	LAPORTE.	O.	R.
Staples, L. c	4	3	Tee', (Capt.) p	2	5
Miller, r f	3	4	Ridgeway, r f	5	2
Thompson, l f	3	4	Vose, l f	1	6
Brusie, p	3	3	Keller, J A, c f	2	6
Dunn, s s	4	3	Meeker L, 1 b	5	3
Rose, c f	2	4	Munday, s s	1	4
Witherill, 2 b	3	2	Meeker, H H, 2 b	3	1
Staples, H, 3 b	3	3	Shattuck, 3 b	4	2
Spain, (Capt.) 1 b	2	1	Heller, J E, c	3	4
	27	30		27	34

INNINGS

	1st	2d	3d	4th	5th	6th	7th	8th	9th	
Excelsior	5	5	7	1	3	1	3	2	3	30
Laporte	4	5	5	5	2	0	5	8	1	34

Time of Game, 2 hours, 55 minutes.
Umpire—Mr. A. J. Eccleston of Excelsior Club.
Scorers—Messrs. V. Nicar of Excelsior Club and L. G. Erb, of Laporte Club.

Although baseball had been played in South Bend since 1860, game reports were considered rather scarce. The first boxscore appeared in the *St. Joseph Valley Register* was on June 28, 1866. In that boxscore, a number of items that appeared are still a part of modern day boxscores. Listed are the runs scored by each player and how many outs were made. There is a breakdown for scoring by innings, time of the game, as well as who the umpires were. It's interesting to note that even though 64 runs were scored, the time of the game did not exceed three hours!

This red and blue baseball and $50 went to the Rough-and-Readys of South Bend for winning the Junior Club Championship during an October 1866 baseball tournament. The tournament was sponsored by the Excelsiors, another South Bend team. As the case for many similar tournaments of that time, there were some additional prizes awarded for individual accomplishments. W.L. Keyzer of the Rough-and-Readys won the prize for being the "quickest runner of bases" and Henry Spain of the Excelsiors claimed the prize for the "best thrower on distance."

Pictured above is George Wyman. While known to many generations as the founder of Wyman's Department Store, he was also a member of the Hoosier Base Ball Club. In 1898, Wyman sponsored a team which carried the name of his store.

TWO

Second Inning

The Legendary Greenstockings

From 1860 to 1877, South Benders enjoyed the sports of baseball with their teams like the Hoosiers, Excelsiors, Rough-and-Readys, Snatchers, Scottas and Headcheeses. In 1878, however, a baseball team was to emerge that was to have an impact on the community as no other had before.

That team was the Greenstockings.

Legend has it that the Greenstockings were founded on a spring day in 1878, under a tree near the Deacon Grocery Store on the corner of Chapin and Napier Streets. Whether that is true or not, we do know that the meeting between John Deacon, Ira Kelly and Henry Peak led to a team that would establish a national baseball reputation for South Bend.

As the case with many early teams, the Greenstocking players also filled the roles of team management. Its first club officers included: Oliver J. Tong, president; Harvey C. Deacon, secretary-treasurer; his brother, John Deacon, manager and captain; and William "Bootsey" Johnson, assistant captain. Members of that first Greenstocking team were Tong, Kelly, Peak, Johnson, the Deacon brothers, Charles Campeau, Fred Rockstroh, Del Kurtz and Ralph Staples.

Once the team was chosen, manager Deacon decided that uniforms and a place to play were the next items of concern. Deacon chose a bright green uniform with dark green stockings (hence the Greenstocking name) and a large "S.B." emblazoned on the left chest.

Team players solicited local businesses for sponsorships to pay for the uniforms. The response was so great that not only would the uniforms be covered, but also there was enough money taken in to build their own ballpark.

E.P. and H.S. Stanfield helped secure a tract of land at the corner of Napier, Thomas and McPherson streets for the tax payment on that land (which was $31.00). Walworth and Lawton supplied all the building materials, including 220 oak posts, 2,300 feet of two-by-four scantling and 13, 700 feet of pine lumber. Local carpenters donated their time after their regular workday to build the park that would be the first enclosed baseball facility in northern Indiana.

On May 21, opening day at Greenstocking Park had finally arrived! A capacity crowd of over 1,500 saw a hard-fought contest, with the hosts dropping a 7-5 decision to a team from Valparaiso, Indiana. According to the news accounts, there were numerous fights and insults traded over the course of the game. Much of that had to do with the taunting of the Greenstockings by the visitors. Apparently, the visitors kept yelling that the S.B. on the uniform of the locals stood for "Silly Boys"—something both the Greenstockings and their fans didn't find funny. The next time the team played at home, the S.B. was gone from the uniform and was replaced by "South Bend."

During that first season of play, the Greenstockings played strong teams from throughout the East and Midwest. Their biggest game of the year though was a June 26 contest in which they hosted the Boston Redstockings of the National League. Although defeated by a score of 21 to 5, Redstockings manager George Wright praised the local players and their playing facility.

The Greenstockings finished the 1878 season with a record of 17-9-1 to take the mythical Indiana State Baseball Championship. During the next two seasons, the Greenstockings saw their number of games drop to 10 in 1879 and then two in 1880. Because the team did not travel extensively, many ballclubs chose not to play them unless it was done on a home-and-home basis. Following the 1880 season, the Greenstockings temporarily disappeared from the baseball scene.

For the 1881–83 seasons, teams like the Hairpins, Eclipses and Liberties attempted to fill the local baseball void. From time to time, John Deacon would get requests to use Greenstocking Park. Most of them would be granted. However, in September 1883, a female team contacted him about playing in the park. Deacon according to the local papers wrote back and told them, "I am obliged to reply that all dates for the South Bend ballgrounds are filled and that the mayor does not permit playing in the city park."

In 1884, the Greenstockings returned to action. They finished that season with a 9-4 mark showing that very little of their playing skills had been lost.

As the 1885 season approached, John Deacon was looking to build a newer and bigger home for his Greenstockings. Securing land on the south side just beyond the city limits, a new Greenstocking Park was built by Theodore Knoblock. With seating of 2,000, it was 500 seats larger than the old park. In 1887, this capacity was enlarged another 500 seats to hold a crowd of 2,500.

Between 1885 and 1888, the Greenstockings clicked off seasons with 23, 28, 26 and 29 wins, respectively. In 1887, the team had their best winning percentage ever, .730. In 1888, the team was invited to be a junior member of professional baseball in the Indiana State League. Although they played a number of games against league members, their final record was not included in the standings.

By 1889, the record for the season stood at 10-9. It was the fewest games played by the team since their "comeback" in 1884. For John Deacon and many of his teammates, they appeared to be ready to pass the baseball torch as the new decade began to turn.

Their contributions, though, continued to be felt and later rewarded when a minor league team would finally call South Bend home shortly after the turn of the century.

1878

FRED. ROCKSTROH. JOHN DEACON. C. CAMPEAU. H. DEACON. HENRY PEAK.
DELL KURTZ. I. J. STAPLES. RALPH STAPLES. WM JOHNSON.

Seen here are members of the 1878 South Bend Greenstockings. One of the major stars from this team was pitcher Del Kurtz (bottom left). Kurtz pitched in all 27 games, logging 240 innings. He also averaged more than 10 assists defensively each time he was on the mound and finished with a team-high 303 for the season. His greatest claim to fame however is that is was reported to be the first curveball pitcher in northern Indiana! During a number of his seasons with the Greenstockings, he could be found listed in the City Directory with his occupation as "Base Ballist."

This is perhaps the only surviving scorecard from the South Bend Greenstockings team. Over July 2, 3 and 4, 1887, the Greenstockings hosted the Cincinnati Shamrocks in a big holiday series. Right before the series began, however, their catcher Jack Grim and pitcher Harry Kelleher got a better financial deal from another team for that same weekend! Strapped for pitching, the steady Del Kurtz was joined by utility infielder Danny Casey as a fellow moundsman for the weekend.

22

GREENSTOCKINGS.

NNINGS....		2	3	4	5	6	7	8	9	At Bat.	Runs.	1st B. Hits.	Total Bases
Johnson, s s.......	0				70			0	0				
Kurtz, l f	0		0					71	71				
Casey, 3d b.......			0		0			1					
Burns, c f.........	5		0										
Staples, 1st b......		0		0		0							
Rockstroh, 2d b....		1		0		0							
Dawson p.........				0			0						
Dobson, r f.......		7			0		0		0				
McAuliff, c........					0		6						
Total Runs......		1	1	1				3 4	5				
Earned Runs.....										Earnd Runs.	1st B. C.B.	Left on B's
1st Base on Hits ...												
1st Base on Errors..												

For catching support, manager John Deacon was given the name of a University of Notre Dame catcher who lived in nearby Michigan City, Indiana. That catcher was James Burns. Both Burns and Casey helped the team to a series win that weekend. For Burns, however, this series would not be the last time he would achieve any notoriety. Later ordained a Holy Cross priest, Burns would go on to serve as the President of Notre Dame from 1919 to 1922!

Just a year after turning down a game request from a female baseball club, a second female club was allowed to play. The ad for this game was from the August 4, 1885 *South Bend Daily Times*. A little over 1,000 fans showed up at Island Park to see the game. The female players ranged in age from 15 to 30 and they played against a picked nine (comprised of top players from several teams) from South Bend. The final score that day was 15 to 7 in favor of the picked nine. A little over 50 years later, South Bend would have its own female baseball team, the Blue Sox of the All American Girls Professional Baseball League.

The 1885 Greenstockings team, winners of 23 games and only ten losses, are pictured from left to right: (front row) McCabe (third base), Johnson (shortstop), and Crockett (left field); (middle row) Casey (left field), Peak (catcher), Kurtz (pitcher), and Rockstroh (second base); (back row) Deacon (manager) Dobson (right field), Staples (first base), Barr (center field), and Fassett (team president).

THREE

Third Inning

Everyone Plays the Game

As the era of the Greenstockings ended, a number of teams during the next few years tried to fill their void. A local league was formed in 1891 featuring teams like the West Ends, East Sides, South Ends and the Centrals. In 1892, the first appearance by teams from local factories started making their appearance on the diamond, most notably of these were teams from Studebakers and Singers. Both of these companies would figure prominently in South Bend baseball circles from the early teens to through the 1940s!

A new form of baseball also made its way to South Bend beginning in 1890. Indoor Baseball, developed in Chicago the year before, was designed to be played during the winter and early spring. It employed a bigger ball and smaller field size, and that made it ideal for roller rinks or large open indoor areas.

Some of the more notable indoor teams from South Bend included the Lum Tums, Iroquois, Indiana Club, Kenwoods, Algonquins and, of course, the Greenstockings.

Promotions and entertainment were used to draw fans to the new indoor game. Joe Matone, a local harpist, provided the musical entertainment for Kenwoods and Lum Tums home games. Players also received perks such as a dollar-off coupon for each winning team member by local barber Henry St. John.

In 1891, the winning team in the South Bend Indoor League won a pennant sponsored by the *South Bend Tribune* newspaper while the second place team got a box of fine cigars from Gaskill's Cigar Store.

The theory behind the game was to allow the baseball players a year-round opportunity to work on the skills. Interestingly enough, after the turn of the century, play of the game was moved outdoors, although it was still referred to as "indoor" baseball. The structure of this game was the basis for the game of softball that is still played on virtually the same size diamond as when it was an indoor game.

The mid-1890s saw the opening of two other baseball diamonds in South Bend. Studebaker Park and Springbrook Park opened for play in 1895 and 1896, respectively. Springbrook Park, which would later change its name to Playland, was the site of baseball games in South Bend for over 50 years.

On September 22, 1895, the Colored Clippers lost to the White Nine by a score of 13 to 11 at Studebaker Park. They were the first local African-American team to be documented in the local paper.

From 1895 through 1897, the South Bend Senators provided the locals with their most stable team to root for since the end of the Greenstocking era. They competed against other local teams and clubs from the Chicago area.

However, it was the arrival of Angus Grant in late 1897 that would prepare South Bend for their next step into professional baseball. Grant was from Defiance, Ohio, and was from a sports-oriented family. His coming to South Bend led to their strongest teams to date. From 1897 through 1902, the South Bend Greens (or Greenstockings) played nearly 100 games a season. They would win more than 60 games each season. A number of their players either had prior professional experience or they used their time in South Bend to prepare them to play pro ball.

Perhaps three of the most notable players from the Greens were pitchers George Mullin and Bailey and infielder Harry Arndt. Arndt and Mullin, after leaving South Bend, would rejoin as teammates in 1902 with the Detroit Tigers of the American League. Arndt had a journeyman career with several major league teams. Mullin was a very successful pitcher with the Tigers and Washington Senators along with Newark and Indianapolis of the Federal League. Bailey pitched in 16 games for Boston in the National League, winning six and losing four.

The Muessel baseball team played in the late 1890s and into the early part of the century. The most notable player on the team was pitcher George Schmalzreid (middle row, far right). He made his debut in 1898 with the Wyman Department Store team as a pitcher-second baseman. What made Schmalzried unique was the fact the he was a one-armed pitcher!

Pictured is an 1890s baseball game in South Bend. It's possible that this photograph was taken at one of the two sites formerly used by the South Bend Greenstockings. The crowd at this park is about as close to the action as you can get without actually being on the field!

Seen here is an early game at Springbrook Park. Opened for play in 1896, this site would host baseball teams in South Bend for over 50 years.

The 1893 Indiana Club Baseball team, pictured from left to right: (front row) Eugene H. Miller (second base), William Rosencrans (catcher), and W.B. Parker (pitcher); (middle row) Horvace V. "Chub" Birdsell (first base), J.M. Studebaker, Jr. (captain / shortstop), Clement Studebaker, Jr. (pitcher), and E. Neff (manager / right field); (back row) Charles H. Harper (center field), George M. Studebaker (left field), and Edson Hickox (third base).

Many different organizations fielded baseball teams in the 1890s. One such team was the Gaelic Baseball team sponsored by the St. Patrick's Church Athletic Club. Team members are pictured from left to right: (front row) A. Lyons, John Hagerty, C.J. (Kealy) hunt, and Tom Sullivan; (second row) J. Cummins, P. Conally, E. Dorna, L. Wills, J. Kelly, and W. McIntyre; (back row) E. Drum, W. Howell, D. Kelly, J. Graham, G. Curry, Jerry Hangerty, W. Donovan, W. McCreary, and F. O'Day.

This is an early tobacco baseball card of George Mullin. He used his time with the South Bend Greens as a springboard to a major league career that was spent mostly with the Detroit Tigers. In a 14-year career, Mullin won 228 major league games. He was a 20 game winner five times, including a high of 29 victories during the 1909 season.

To tha Honorable Mayor and Common Council of the City of South
Bend, Ind.

Gentlemen,-

We the undersigned members of the Algonquin Club and
citizens of the city of South Bend, Ind. petition your honorable
body for permision to use the rink for the purpose of playing
indoor Baseball. Your petitioners will be responsible for all
damages to the property that may occur, and your petitioners will
ever pray.

This 1899 petition by the Algonquin Indoor Baseball team to the South Bend City Council asked for use of the "Rink" for their baseball games. Most noteworthy on the list of petitioners is the signature of H. (Harry) Arndt on the right hand column. Arndt played baseball (indoor and the outdoor variety) in South Bend in the 1890s before joining the Detroit Tigers in 1902.

Harry Arndt's baseball card when he was with the minor league team from Providence. Arndt was the first native-born player from South Bend to play in the major leagues. Born in South Bend in 1879, Arndt broke into the majors in 1902 with the Detroit Tigers after a successful run on the South Bend sandlots. According to the newspapers, he cracked a triple in his first game and received a standing ovation from the Detroit fans when he went to bat his final time that day. Arndt played 271 games for the Tigers, Baltimore Orioles and St. Louis Cardinals between 1902 and 1907. Arndt later came back to South Bend to play for and manage the 1912 Central League team. Arndt hit .302 that year, but it was of very little help as his team finished 41-88, last place in the 12-team league. He would later go on to help found the professional South Michigan League (which South Bend played in during 1914–15). In March of 1921, Arndt passed away just after his 42nd birthday.

FOUR

Fourth Inning

Professional and Factory

League Ball

In 1903, after his successful run with the semi-pro South Bend Greens, manager Angus Grant was chosen to lead the City's first foray into professional baseball.

That season, South Bend became a charter member of the newly formed Central League, a Class B circuit. The nickname chosen for this team was—yes—the Greenstockings! Immediately that first season South Bend was a strong contender for the pennant as they racked up 88 wins, good for a second place finish. The next two seasons saw the club finish third with win totals of 75 and 77 in 1904 and 1905, respectively.

Grant would lead the South Bend team for the first seven seasons of its existence in the Central League. He was gone in 1910, but returned for the 1911 season. During his tenure, Grant chalked up a total of 504 wins, still the top win total for any South Bend minor league manager's career.

In 1910, the local fans were given a taste of a winner as their South Bend Broncho team copped the Central League pennant that year with a 88-50 record. That team was run by player-manager Eddie Wheeler.

At least five of the players from this team either had major league experience or would soon after the 1910 season make their way to the big leagues. Among them was pitcher Ed Smith, winner of 22 games. Outfielder Harry Welchonce led South Bend with a batting average of .315. Another outfielder, Max Carey hit .293 and had 36 stolen bases. Carey would go on to have a long major league career (with mostly the Pittsburgh Pirates) and was later voted into the baseball Hall of Fame. Joining Carey on the Pirates after the 1910 season was shortstop Alex McCarthy. A slick fielder, McCarthy had 446 assists in 1910. And finally, Ben Koehler, who had many ties to amateur and professional baseball in South Bend, hit .260 and had 32 stolen bases.

Following the 1910 season, the next two were not so fortunate for the South Bend team. The low mark was in 1912 when the team finished last in the Central League with a record of 41-88! In 1913, there was no professional baseball in South Bend, but that year saw the beginning of strong factory-sponsored clubs in the mid-teens.

For 1914 and 1915, South Bend again returned to professional baseball, this time as a member of the Southern Michigan League, a Class D circuit. In 1914, they team played well in the league but in 1915, South Bend dominated the first half season of play. So much so, that the league folded and did not finish out the year. Rather than try to re-organize the league for 1916, it was back to the Central League for South Bend in 1916 and 1917.

The teams, however, could not recapture the interest of those earlier seasons and in July 1917, the South Bend franchise was transferred to Peoria, Illinois.

Although professional baseball had a downturn in the mid to late teens, that was not the case for amateur and factory teams who flourished during that same period of time. Factories in South Bend like Singers, Studebakers and Olivers had company teams that played during the week. On weekends, and they all had what amounted to all-star teams that played in the local Industrial Baseball League.

That same time frame saw the emergence of powerful African-American League teams as well. Locally, the South Bend Colored Giants would be managed by Ted Strong, Sr. One of his sons, Ted Strong, Jr. was born in South Bend in 1917 and would go on the be an outstanding star in the Negro Leagues. Strong, who made Negro League All-Star teams at a variety of positions, is thought to be one of the best athletes to ever play in the League. His athletic skills were not confined to baseball either. Strong, Jr. was one of the earliest members of the Harlem Globetrotters basketball team.

As the teens drew to a close, South Bend was readying itself for the biggest explosion of baseball that the community had ever known!

South Bend's first entry into professional baseball was in 1903 as a member of the Central League. Team members are pictured from left to right: (up front) Red Cogswell (outfield), and Heinie Tieman (catcher); (seated) Elmer Moffitt (pitcher), George "Snips" Schafer (pitcher), Ed Smith (pitcher), Danny Ream (pitcher), Cecil Ferguson (pitcher), "Cuppy" Groeschow (shortstop), "Goat" Anderson (outfield), "Aunt 'Lil" Sager (third base), Alva Spangler (firstbase), Eddie Coffey (outfield), and Angus Grant (second base).

The Whitecaps were an amateur team that played in and around South Bend around 1908–1911. Although most of the identities of this team are not known, one individual on this team can be spotted. Paul Frankel (back row, second from left) would go on to be involved with local baseball for nearly 60 years. However, he is best known as "Pop" Frankel. Many of his former players in South Bend who later went on to coach or manage were given a good foundation in baseball under his direction.

BUSH, DETROIT

Here is a tobacco card of Owen "Donie" Bush. After playing with South Bend in 1907, Bush was well on his way to a major league career, mostly with the Detroit Tigers. He was a slick-fielding shortstop. A native Hoosier born in Indianapolis, Bush would play in his hometown near the end of his playing days. He later owned the Indianapolis team, and the stadium that they played in was renamed as "Bush Stadium."

In 1909, a first occured for the local minor league team as two brothers appeared on the same roster. Ray Wells (left) was a catcher. In 1909, he got into 75 games and hit for an average of .221. Brother Robert was a pitcher. However, being a young pitcher on a veteran staff, Robert only got into one game in 1909, pitching three and one-third innings—and his batterymate was his brother! In 1910, Ray was back with South Bend as a catcher-outfielder and he hit .280. It's not known whether Robert ever played professionally again.

When South Bend won its first minor league pennant, these were the players who led them to the top. Team members are pictured from left to right: (front row) Lindsay (pitcher), Craven (rightfield), McCarthy (shortstop), and Kroy (left field); (middle row) Wells (catcher), Wheeler (manger / thirdbase); Coffey (centerfield), Smith (pitcher), and Watson (catcher); (top row) Connors (first base), Corbitt (pitcher), Koehler (second base), Moffitt (pitcher), and Meyers (pitcher).

With an 88-50 record, South Bend won the Central League pennant. In September, the official presentation was made to the team at Springbrook Park in South Bend. In the upper left hand

portion of the photograph, note the "Bull Durham" sign.

In 1910 pitcher John Henry Meyers was cut from the South Bend Central League team. However, a few days later manager Eddie Wheeler rethought his decision and brought Meyers back to the team. An average pitcher during his Central League career, he proved to be much the same during the 1910 season in South Bend where he won 14 games and also lost 14 games. One game, though, put Meyers in the local record book with a mark that still stands today. On July 13, hurling against the Zanesville Potters, Meyers threw a 21-inning, complete game winning by a score of 1 to 0!

SOUTH BEND.

	AB	R	H	SH	SB	O	A	E
Wells	0	0	0	0	0	6	6	0
Wheeler	9	0	3	1	0	8	5	0
Welchonce	.8	1	3	0	0	3	1	0
Connors ..	..8	0	1	1	0	22	0	0
Carey	8	0	3	0	0	2	2	1
Kroy	8	0	3	0	2	0	0	0
McCarthy	7	0	2	0	0	6	5	1
Holmes	8	0	2	0	0	9	0	0
Myers	8	0	1	0	0	1	3	0
Total	84	1	18	2	2	63	22	2

ZANESVILLE.

	AB	R	H	SH	SB	O	A	E
Baggan	.7	0	1	0	0	1	0	
Crowder ..	..6	0	2	2	1	6	6	
Hellinger	...17	0	0	0	0	4	0	
McNiece	..7	0	0	0	0	1	0	
Donahue ..	..6	0	2	0	0	2	2	
Herold	..8	0	2	0	0	2	3	
Swartling	8	0	2	0	0	29	2	
O'Brien	8	0	1	0	0	13	6	
Jones	..8	0	1	0	0	2	6	
Total	65	0	11	2	1	62	25	

SCORE BY INNINGS.

South Bend ....0 0 0 0 0 0 0.0 0 0 0 0 0 0 0 0 0 0 1—1   18 2

Zanesville .. ..0 0 0 0 0 0 0 0 0 0 0 0 0 0 0 0 0 0 0—0   10 3

Hits made off Myers, 11; Jones, 18.

Struck out by Jones—Carey, Holmes and Myers.

Twobase hits—Swartling, O'Brien, Holmes and Donahue.

Bases on balls—Baggan, Donahue and Kroy.

Double play—Myers, Wheeler, Connors, Donahue and Swartling.

Left on bases—Zanesville, 1; South Bend, 1.

Time of game—3:26. Umpire—Newhouse.

On July 13, 1910, South Bend and Zanesville locked-up in quite a pitchers duel, one that never seemed it was going to end. John Henry Meyers of South Bend and a spitballer named Jones from Zanesville matched zeroes for 20 straight innings. In the bottom of the 21st inning, South Bend loaded the bases and then shortstop Alex McCarthy drove a single into the outfield for a thrilling 1-0 South Bend win. Meyers gave up only 11 hits and only two walks while striking out 11. While Meyers' 21-inning shutout is a record that still stands today in the South Bend books, Cack Henley, a pitcher with San Francisco of the Pacific Coast League, just a year before tossed a 1-0, 24-inning shutout against Oakland. This is how the boxscore appeared in the *South Bend Daily Times* on July 14, 1910.

South Bend manger Eddie Wheeler was happy to acquire the pitching services of Ted Corbitt for the 1910 season. Corbitt was a solid addition to the staff and compiled a record of 16-7 for the pennant winning team. Just a day after teammate John Henry Meyers' 21-inning shutout victory, local baseball fans were treated to a no-hitter by Corbitt! The Zanesville team—victims the day before—lost the first game of a doubleheader to South Bend by a score of 5 to 2. Corbitt took the mound in game two. Neither team could dent the plate. Darkness began to fall as the game went into the ninth and 10th innings. Umpires decided that the 11th would be the final inning of play. Both clubs went down in order. At the end, Corbitt had tossed an 11-inning no-hitter and ended-up with a 0-0 no decision!

South Bend shortstop Alex McCarthy stretches to snare a linedrive during a game. McCarthy knocked in the only run in South Bend's 21-inning shutout of Zanesville in July of 1910. Many local fans knew of his playing ability before he came to the local Central League club. McCarthy had played college baseball at the University of Notre Dame. After the 1910 season, his contract was sold to the Pittsburgh Pirates where he spent most of his major league career.

Ed Smith started his professional baseball career in 1899 with Kokomo in the Indiana State League. However, he would play a key role during the many seasons of minor league baseball in South Bend. His first stop in South Bend was from 1908 to 1911. In 1909 and 1910, he was one of the team workhorses, working 304 and 305 innings each season. In 1910, he won 22 games as South Bend captured the Central League pennant. He left for several season, but returned as the owner-player-manager of South Bend's Michigan State League team. In 1916, he oversaw the renovation of the baseball diamond at Springbrook Park. And, during the 1916 and 1917 seasons, he brought South Bend back into the Central League. For many years after his retirement from baseball, Smith worked for the South Bend Schools in the Buildings and Grounds department.

When South Bend entered the Central League in 1903, it seemed that not a year would go by that you could not find Elmer "Sappy" Moffitt on its pitching staff. Moffitt, whose family was from nearby New Carlisle, Indiana, owns countless pitching records for South Bend minor league baseball. Those records include most games pitched (164), most innings pitched (1,340 1/3), wins (95), losses (60), strikeouts (765), shutouts (12), and one-hitters (3). Moffitt pitched for South Bend from 1903 to 1906 and then again from 1909 to 1911. Three successive seasons he topped the 20-win mark (1903–05).

Eddie Wheeler had some big shoes to fill. When he was signed as player-manager for South Bend's Central League team, he was replacing Angus Grant. It was Grant who led South Bend into professional baseball in 1903 after years of successful semi-pro teams. But Wheeler was up to the task and in his first season running the team, did something Grant was unable to do—win a pennant! With an 88-50 record, his team was the Central League champs. Besides his managerial contributions, Wheeler held down third base for his team, hit .263 and stole 20 bases.

In 1912, the South Bend Base Ball Association sold shares of stock in the local minor league team. The team had been in the Central League since its inception in 1903. Despite hiring Harry Arndt, a native South Bender and former major leaguer as manager, the team finished last in the 12-team league with a 44-88 record. Local business F.W. Mueller was the owner of this certificate. In 1987, an old Singer sewing machine was purchased, and stuck under one of the drawers was this certificate, which had been neatly folded and forgotten for many years.

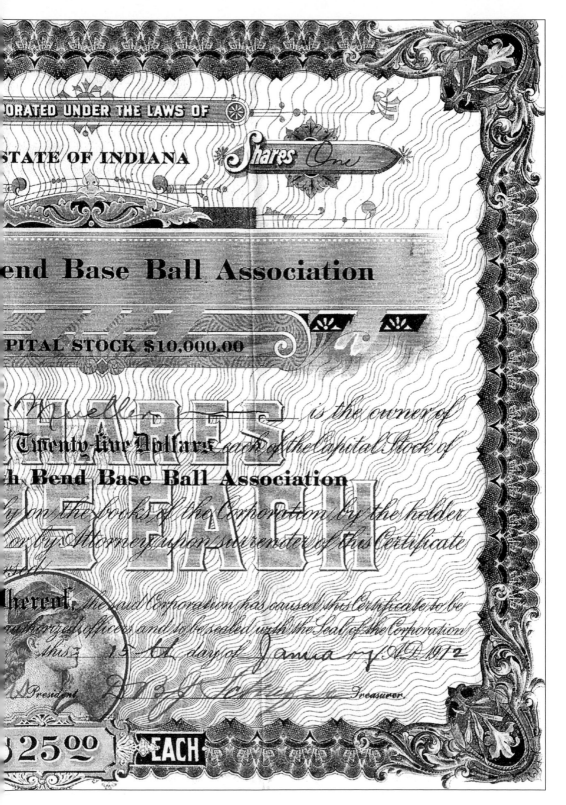

ORATED UNDER THE LAWS OF

STATE OF INDIANA

Shares One

end Base Ball Association

PITAL STOCK $10,000.00

is the owner of

Twenty-five Dollars each of the Capital Stock of

h Bend Base Ball Association

on the books of the Corporation by the holder

or by Attorney upon surrender of this Certificate

hereof, the said Corporation has caused this Certificate to be

authorized officers and to be sealed with the Seal of the Corporation

this 15th day of January A.D. 1912

President

Treasurer

$25.00 EACH

In 1913, The Singer Manufacturing Company decided to enter the local baseball competition on a big-time basis. As a number of companies came together to form a local Industrial Baseball League, Singers went one better by building their own ballpark! Seating some 1,500 fans, Singer Park opened in 1913. Each department at Singers would field a baseball team for weekday games and on the weekends, an all-star team taken from the best of all those teams would take on other factory all-start teams.

Singer Park was one of the top sites in the teens and 1920s for some of the premier barnstorming baseball teams in the United States. Clubs like the House of David and major league teams like the St. Louis Cardinals played exhibition games against the Singer team. In this photograph, you can see a rail fence in front of the bleachers, which would be used early on to tie horse-drawn carriages that brought fans to the game.

The first of three pennants won by Singers in the local Industrial Baseball League, the 1913 flag was presented in August and raised high above the fence at Singer Park. It would be a sight that the Singer fans grew accustomed to through 1915.

For the first three years of the local Industrial Baseball League, the Singer team dominated play, winning the pennant in each of those seasons (1913–1915). Pictured here, from left to right, is the 1913 team: (front row) Ring, Ziedler, Zielinski, Wartha, Davidison, and Gruber; (back row) Segety (manager), Moore, Spair, Schafer, McDowell, Werntz, Vargo, Connors, and Lentz. This team took their first pennant with a record of 12 wins and 3 losses.

Pictured is the covered grandstand at Singer Park. The park was opened in 1913 and a short while afterwards a cover was constructed over the grandstand. Seating capacity of the park was 1,500 when it opened and within two years, the top capacity was 2,500. The park also had an area where carriages, and later automobiles, could be pulled in to watch the game action.

When Singer Park was built in 1913, it had many amenities on its grounds including a clubhouse (pictured here) where both home and visiting players could change. Features like this allowed many top traveling teams the same treatment that they would otherwise find in larger cities and ballparks. At the lower left of this photograph is the ticket window of Singer Park.

tz-Mgr Connors-1B Martin-P. Edgren-P. Hudak-C Baker-C Bacon-C.F. McQuaid
Ring-P. Zielinski-2B Capt. Vargo-L.F. Aftowski-S.S. Sullivan-3B Zietler-R.F.
THE SINGER BASE BALL TEAM
CHAMPIONS MANUFACTURERS LEAGUE 1915.

For three straight years, the Singer team topped all teams in the local factory league. Renamed the Manufacturers League in 1915, the name change didn't change the results as the Singer team finished as champions. Members of that team are pictured from left to right: (front row) Ring (pitcher), Zielinski (captain / second base), Vargo (left field), Aftowski (shortstop), Sullivan (third base), and Zietler (right field); (back row) Lentz (manager), Connors (first base), Martin (pitcher), Edgren (pitcher), Hudak, Baker (catcher), Bacon (center field), and McQuaid. Although Singers continued to compete in future factory league play, their team would never again dominate like they did during the first three seasons.

For nearly two decades, Frank "Snooder" Aftowski would be on the local baseball scene. Many of those years were spent with the Singer baseball club. Here he is pictured on the "Singer Special" which was a train bound for the annual tournament in the east that would pit all the Singer factory champs against each other for the overall factory crown. After his playing days, "Snooder" was always working with young ballplayers in South Bend. He was the manager of the Post 357 American League state champs in 1937.

Members of the 1913 Singer Industrial League Base Ball champs admire their trophy that had just been presented to the team by C. A. Clauer. C.N. Fassett, Editor-in-Chief of the *South Bend News Times*, presented the pennant to the team.

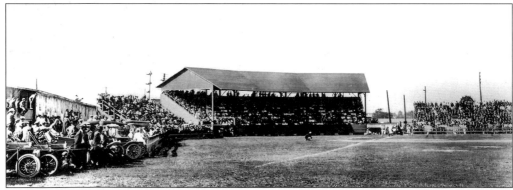

Seen here is a packed grandstand at Singer Park in the late teens. Note the standing fans at the very top of the covered grandstand and at the right of the photograph. The wheels of automobiles that were allowed to pull into and park on the Singer grounds can be seen very close to the playing field.

While baseball teams were having great success all over the city, South Bend High School struggled with having a team. Not that the interest wasn't there, but there were no other school close by for them to play. Competition was then limited to games between the various classes at the high school. Pictured are the members of the 1918 school champs. On that team is Rudolph Ash, the first African-American baseball player at the high school.

This is a graphic from *The Interlude*, a South Bend High School publication. Even though there was not any outside competition for the local high school team to play, they played an enthusiastic interclass schedule.

FIVE

Fifth Inning

The Golden Years

Without a doubt, the richest and most active years in South Bend baseball history was the period between 1920 and the late 1940s. Factory teams, fraternal organizations, schools, semi-pro teams and indoor teams had games going seven days a week. Directories were run in the local newspapers listing all the local baseball contacts in the city!

Stanley Coveleski, former star pitcher with the Cleveland Indians, finished up his major league career in 1928 with the New York Yankees, and in 1929 chose South Bend for his home until his death in 1984. Coveleski pitched on a number of local teams after coming to South Bend and also spent time giving baseball playing advice to youngsters.

Interestingly enough during this time period, there was only one season with a professional minor league team. In 1932, the South Bend Twins joined the Central League, but given the difficult economic times, the team folded in July.

Yet, the local baseball fans came out consistently supporting all of the other teams in town. A new baseball park opened on the south side of town in 1929 by the Studebaker Corporation. Lippincott Park, as it would be named, would be used by teams all the way into the 1950s.

There was some discussion in 1938 to bring a Negro League franchise to South Bend. Many times Negro League teams would play exhibition games against the locals, or two Negro League teams might play a regular season game in South Bend. But, since the best park in town (Lippincott) was controlled by Studebaker's, that idea was soon dropped.

Despite that effort falling through, the baseball fires in South Bend burned strongly through the late 1940s.

Like the Singer baseball team in the teens, the Studebaker Corporation took to the forefront in the early 1920s. The company would have the various automotive divisions playing in the company league during the week and on the weekend. The best of those players formed the Studebaker Athletics. This team represented the M. & A. Division.

Another one of the Studebaker company division teams was the one that represented the Foundry. Traditionally, this team was comprised of African-American players. Their players were not included on the weekend Studebaker Athletic team; however, members of the Foundry team would play as the South Bend Colored Giants.

The General Office at Studebakers was represented in the company league, although few of their players would participate on the weekend team.

Another strong company league team was represented by Plant One. They consistently held their own against either the Foundry or M. & A. Division teams.

V. KIMBLE   HERB CLEWELL.   F.A. BRENNER   G. PRETZ
THE SEASON OPENERS

(*above*) Pictured is the 1924 season opener for the Studebaker Company baseball teams. From left to right are Studebaker officials H.V.Kimble, Herb Clewell, F.A. Brenner and G. Pretz. On opening days, vitually everyone from the Studebaker Company turned out for this festive occasion.

CLEWELL AND BECKER
"OFFICIAL" UMPS

(*left*) Also from the 1924 opener, umpires Clewell and Becker try to make themselves heard through megaphones before the start of the games.

With McKeun at the far left, Studebaker official F.A. Brenner takes a good healthy swing in a program ceremony in 1924. H.V. Kimble served as both catcher and umpire.

C.A. LIPPINCOTT
J.M. BECKER
MR. DENISON
H. CLEWELL
W.K. STUDEBAKER
THE PUT-OUT
F.A. BRENNER
C. PRETZ

More Studebaker officials take their turn on the ball diamond. From left to rights are C.A. Lippincott, J.M. Becker, Mr. Denison, Clewell, W.K. Studebaker, Pretz and Brenner. Many of the early Studebaker games were played at Springbrook Park (later Playland). Note the ad for the Hotel Jefferson high above the action on the field.

Here is a view of the grandstand at Lippincott Park in South Bend. Built by the Studebaker Corporation and dedicated in 1929, the park held a capacity crowd of 2,500. As time went on the seating was increased to 5,000.

Here is the view looking out toward centerfield at Lippincott Park. According to the newspaper accounts, the deepest portion of centerfield went back 475 feet!

Players from the Studebaker Stampers baseball club, *circa* 1927, are pictured from left to right: (front row) Walling, Shaw, Harrel, Moffitt, Brown, Whitten and Franks; (back row) Wasson, Beach, Shay, Camer, Werntz, Terwillinger, Newman, Wamsley and Bartz. The team competed in the company Twilight League.

A typical ad used by the South Bend Independents baseball team in the mid-1920s. This particular ad is from the *South Bend News-Times* on July 11, 1926. The opponent for that day, the Chicago Union Giants (an African-American team) had for many years been a good draw in South Bend.

Indoor baseball (now played outside) was still popular in the mid-1920s. Here are the members of the Oliver Chilled Plow Assembly Department team. They finished second in the company league with a 9-3 record. Other department teams competing in their league were Time

Keeping, Stock, Plant No. 2, and Accounting and Assembly. One of the top hitters and pitchers on this team was Matthew Nowak who is pictured on the top row, fourth from the left.

Pictured is an early 1920s baseball card of Stanley Coveleski. After a great career in the major league with four different teams, Coveleski retired to South Bend. For a number of years and pitched on local semi-pro teams, like the South Bend Indians, Silver Edgers and M.R. Falcons.

Stanley Coveleski not only helped coach and on occasion, but also the mound to help with the pitching chores or provide a draw for the 1929 M.R. Falcon baseball club. Pictured from left to right: (front row) Pat Pilarski, Jack Schoen, Ed Marshall, Joe Savoldi, Casimer Struck, and Hardy Clemens; (back row) Stanley Chelminiak, Gene Ziolkowski, Casmier Bolka, Eddie Hanyzewski, Ben Piotrowski, Kenny Caron, Hank Meilstroup, Bernie Witucki, and Heinie Florkowski. Coveleski and Erv Pilarski were the only two from the team who are not pictured.

A July 2, 1929 ad from the *South Bend News-Times* encourages all to come out to see Stanley Coveleskie (the "e" was used much of his major league career and on-and-off after his retirement to South Bend). The game featured Coveleskie pitching for the hometown South Bend Indians against a top Negro League team, the Detroit Stars.

BASEBALL
PLAYLAND PARK
WEDNESDAY, 6 P. M.
DETROIT STARS
vs.
S. B. INDIANS

Congressman Oscar De Priest guest of honor.
Doubleheader Sunday
St. Joe A. C. vs. Mich. City
1 P. M.
FT. WAYNE vs. INDIANS
3 P. M.
Coveleskie-Sullivan
.Admission 50c

One of the Studebaker baseball teams takes time to pose for a group photograph, *circa* 1929.

Umpire Norris "Gadget" Ward was an outstanding athlete in his playing days and he kept his involvement with sports, in particular baseball for decades. Starting in the late 1930s, he umpired amateur and semi-pro baseball games and became an Umpire-In-Chief for the All American Girls Professional Baseball League. He later served as the commissioner for the Michiana Amateur Baseball League, a college age and older league that began play in South Bend and surrounding area in 1975.

Another active front in baseball during this time was on the high school level. Although the number of scheduled games was not as great as the teams of today play, a lot of local rivalry existed. Here is the 1928 South Bend High School that compiled a record of 5 wins 4 losses. Team members are pictured from left to right: (front row) Joe Woodka, Howard McDaniels, Dwight Ritter, Philip Sherman, Coblentz, Witucki, Russel Hawk (captain), and G. Golabowski; (middle row) Ernest Szekley, Ernest Borror, Tilden Forst, William Case, Brooker, and Oscar Zoss. (back row) Bud Fisher, Turner, Ben Curtis, Coach Burnham, and Ben Koehler. Curtis was the first documented African-American varsity baseball player at a South Bend high school.

In the mid-1930s, the baseball program at South Bend High School continued to grow. During that time there coach was a man by the name of John Wooden. Like many high school coaches, he often handled a number of sports during the year. Basketball was his other sport of choice. In fact, few people are aware that Wooden ever coached anything but basketball. The South Bend John Wooden is the same man who would later gain fame as the "Wizard of Westwood," the legendary head basketball coach from UCLA. Here is a photograph of Wooden and one of his baseball teams at South Bend High School. Pictured from left to right: (front row) Weaver, Shaw, Moroszowski, and Doerts; (middle row) Litherland, Blakla, Donaldson, Benz, Sadural, Cooper, Lawler, Flanagan, Pawelski, and Mikula; (back row) Mor, Urnson, Bredmus, White, Koehler, Nowicki, Wooden, Hans, Hickey, Janicki, Regan, Marling, and Keller.

In 1932, minor league baseball again beckoned to South Bend. However, the organization behind the entry into the Central League (which South Bend had been a charter member of back in 1903) was not very strong on the business end. This is a copy of the scorecard used by the South Bend Twins during their brief re-entry into the Central League.

To help with the pitching, the Twins acquired the services of former major league pitcher Jack Wisner. According to the newspapers, Wisner would work with the young pitchers on the staff and from time to time, fill in on the mound as well.

Jess Altenburg was selected as the field manager for the South Bend Twins in 1932. He also had a role as far as keeping the financial records for the ballclub. When the team ket losing and bills were not getting paid, Altenburg was let go, but it was too late to save the local franchise.

Outfielder Whitey Felber was the last of three managers during the ill-fated 1932 season. That year, the South Bend team that had just re-entered the Central League would not finish the season. The club played well under Felber, but it could not overcome its financial losses.

Infielder Ray Prehn was another member of the ill-fated South bend Twins team. Like many other ballplayers, Prehn had hoped a solid season might get him a look by a major league team or at the very least, it was hoped that a good year would allow his minor league team to sell his contract to a higher level team. The financial difficulties by South Bend, led to organized baseball banning any future attempts at fielding a pro team in the city. That ban was rescinded in 1937.

One of the local players who got an opportunity to play with the Twins in 1932 was Andy Bakos. An outstanding athlete at South Bend High School, he had reasonable success with the local team until it folded. Afterwards for a number of years, Bakos could be found playing for a number of different teams on the South Bend diamonds.

Indoor baseball (now mostly played outside) was a draw for male and female players alike. Companies like Wilson Brothers, Studebakers, and Olivers had female indoor ball clubs who would compete within and outside the plant. Pictured here is catcher Dorothy Swiatowy.

In 1937, Pulaski Post 357 became the first South Bend team to win the Indiana American Legion championship. One of the coaches on this team was Frank "Snooder" Aftowski, a former star with the Singer baseball team in the local Industrial League. Members of that championship team are pictured from left to right: (front row) Joe Rodick, Leo Sobieralski, Camile VanDeWalle, Harry Dlugosz, Clem Sobieralski, and Ben Adamski; (middle row) Joseph Hecklinski, Ernie Hecklinski, Marion Rejer, and Matt Osowski; (back row) Coach Witucki, Pete Rataczyk, Ed Hanyzewski, Ed Rzepnicki, Ervin Wroblewski, Matt Grembowicz, Ed Talboom, and Aftowski.

During the summer of 1946, the American Legion Post 50 team from South bend compiled a record of 13-6. Team members, pictured from left to right, are Harold Jones, jim Patetrson, Phil Potts, Louis Frank, Dave Coquillard, John Knox, John Mull, Jack Morrical, and Bill Balok.

In the mid-1940s, one could not talk about local pitchers without the name of Glenn Hankins coming up. Hankins, better know by his nickname of "lefty," was the ace of the John Adams High School pitching staff during that era. Here is a photograph of Hankins in mid-delivery.

After getting quite a bit of attention with the baseball prowess at Lincoln Junior High School in South Bend, Dick and Don Truex, red-haired identical twins, always turned heads when they played baseball at Adams High School. This photograph shows Don (right) and Dick when they were both in the Philadelphia Phillies farm system.

In 1946, pitcher Bob Hartman was a key pitcher of the James Whitcomb Riley High School pitching staff. Here is a shot of Hartman showing his fastball delivery that baffled many Northern Indiana hitters.

This birds-eye view shows the Riley varsity baseball team in action at Studebaker Park. Located near the school, this area was wide-open, even in the outfield. The rightfielder in this photograph is just a short toss from the neighborhood homes!

In the 1940s and 1950s, there were two South Bend Catholic schools that also put baseball teams on the local diamonds. Pictured here at the right is Wawrzyniak, a pitcher with the Central Catholic baseball team in 1948.

In 1946, South Bend Catholic fielded its first varsity baseball team. Members that first year are pictured from left to right: (front row) C. Holmes, W. Klota, R. Thilman, S. Przestwor, R. Barnhart, L. Budzinski, and E. Prawat; (back row) J. Ryback, E. Karczewski, R. Balka, E. Dobrzykowski, H. Bankowski, and W. Santa (manager).

Six

Sixth Inning
The All Americans
Come to Town

In December of 1942, there was an article that appeared in the local newspaper telling about a women's baseball league that was being formed by Chicago Cub owner William Wrigley. Wrigley's plan was to locate the teams in this league in cities and towns in the Midwest where they might provide entertainment for all those folks who were on the home front working during World War II.

More importantly for Wrigley, however, was the idea that if major league baseball would have to suspend play or cut short the season (as they did in World War I), these female teams could then be used to draw people to the major league parks.

To test the interest in his idea, Wrigley put up fifty percent of the money per team for a four-team league. It was up to the interested communities to raise the other fifty percent. After much local discussion, South Bend announced that they would join the cities of Kenosha and Racine, Wisconsin and Rockford, Illinois for that first season of play in 1943. It's interesting to note that when the league suspended play after the 1954 season, the only remaining original teams were South Bend and Rockford.

The game played by these women at the outset of the league was a hybrid between baseball and softball. The pitchers threw underhand, using a 12-inch softball. The bases were shorter than a regulation size baseball diamond, yet longer than a softball field. Runners were allowed to take lead-offs as in baseball. And, most importantly, the uniforms worn by the players were skirts!

One factor that Wrigley wanted to sell was the femininity of the league players. It was his feeling that the softball players at that time might be good ballplayers, but many appeared to be too masculine for his idea. Wrigley's skirted ballplayers would also attend charm school and have team chaperones.

Wrigley's involvement was short-lived once he saw that major league baseball would not shut down. Arthur Meyerhoff, an advertising executive in Chicago, took over the league from Wrigley and led it to its greatest success. Now known as the All American Girls Professional Baseball League, the league still controlled player allocation to keep play in the league balanced. It was thought that the more competitive the play, the more return fans that there would be.

A number of the cities in the league developed baseball program for girls. In 1947, the South Bend Recreation Department ran a 12-team Girls Baseball League!

The last few years of the league, many of the franchises wanted to control their own destiny. No more league spring training, equal advertising or balanced player allocation. By 1954, some teams were living day to day and at the end of that season, league officials voted to suspend play for 1955. The thinking was that a year of regrouping would be needed for the league to come back—except for a touring team that traveled.

In the late 1950s, the All American Girls Professional Baseball League has run its course. During the life cycle of the league, the pitching style went from underhand to sidearm to overhand, and the size of the ball went from 12 to nine inches. The game at its end was played on a field just slightly smaller than a regular baseball diamond.

Even today in South Bend, there are many people who recall going to Blue Sox games at Playland Park. Recalling the teams' divisional title and two championships along with player names like Betsy Jochum, Lib Mahon, Jean Faut, and Mary Baker brings a smile to their face.

The first home field for the South Bend Blue Sox was Bendix Field. They used this field from 1943 to 1945. As each season went by, the Blue Sox drew more and more fans. After the 1945 season it was decided a new home would be needed to meet the growing attendance.

The South Bend Blue Sox of 1946 are pictured from left to right: (front row) Daisy Junor, Viola Thompson, Dorothy Naum, Marie Kruckel, Senaida Wirth, and Jean Faut; (middle row) Inez Voyce, Marge Stefani, Joyce Hill, Betty Luna, Bonnie Baker, and Lillian Luckey; (back row) Jenny Romatowski, Betsy Jochum, Phyllis Koehn, D.C. Grant (manager), Lucille Moore (chaperone), Mona Denton, and Elizabeth Mahon.

In 1946, the South Bend Blue Sox moved into their new home at Playland Park. Playland had been a baseball home for many South Bend teams since 1896. The Blue Sox would play at this park through the final season of 1954. A fervent Blue Sox fan kept this scorecard, noting not only the final score (the Blue Sox lost to the Grand Rapids Chicks, 7-0), but also the date, starting time and the attendance. Over 5,300 attended that first game at Playland for the Blue Sox, and that set a new game attendance mark for the team. They later drew better than 7,000 for a game to shatter the opening game mark.

MAY 26, 1946

"GRAND RAPIDS CHICKS"

Official Score Card

8:30 P.M.

OPENING GAME

SOUTH BEND
BLUE SOX

MEMBER

ALL AMERICAN
GIRLS' BASEBALL LEAGUE

NEW HOME

PLAYLAND PARK

SOUTH BEND, INDIANA

Presented with our compliments - for your better enjoyment of Girls' Baseball.

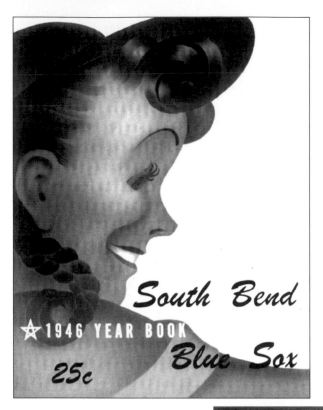

This is the program cover used by the 1946 Blue Sox. As with all the teams of the All American Girls Professional Baseball League, all advertising and promotional items looked identical on the outside. For the programs, the graphic for all the teams was the same; the only change would be in the color. For the Blue Sox, the color of the player was, well, of course—blue!

The field announcer for the Blue Sox home games was Joe Boland, a well-known radio sportscaster on both the local and national level. While many people associate him with broadcasts of Notre Dame football, Boland also loved baseball. His work with the Blue Sox led him to a rather unique experience in 1943. The All-American Girls Professional Baseball League held an All-Star game in Chicago that summer. What made the game historic is that it was the first night game played at Wrigley Field. Portable lights were brought in for that contest and Boland served as the announcer that night!

D.C "Chet" Grant managed the Blue Sox in 1946 and 1947. His first season, he took his team to a 70-42 record. In his youth, Grant played baseball and football at South Bend High School and later went on to quarterback for the University of Notre Dame football team. He was a writer for the *South Bend News-Times* as well.

Blue Sox runner Betsy Jochum attempts to leg-out an infield hit in 1946. Jochum is the owner of the all-time single season mark for most singles with 120 in 1944. That same year, she also won the batting title with an average of .296 and stole 128 bases!

The Blue Sox ARE GOOD
For South Bend Because . . .

The South Bend Blue Sox, Incorporated, is a NON-PROFIT corporation, organized to bring summer-long major-league girls professional baseball to South Bend.

The name of South Bend is publicized daily in seven other member-cities of the All-America League. National publicity about the league and the Blue Sox puts South Bend in the spotlight.

The Blue Sox are currently supporting several amateur girls leagues, playing girls baseball, on South Bend playgrounds — with all expenses paid by the South Bend Sox, Incorporated. Further extensions of these leagues are planned for the future.

All profits earned by the Blue Sox MUST go to the promotion and improvement of recreational facilities in South Bend.

SO . . . your support — and that of your friends—will make the enterprise successful. By attending games at the new home of the Blue Sox—**Playland Park** with your family and friends, you . . .

Help the Blue Sox
Help South Bend

1947 OFFICIAL SCHEDULE

South Bend Blue Sox

of the

ALL-AMERICAN GIRLS BASEBALL LEAGUE

●

PLAYLAND PARK

Home of The Blue Sox

●

Office: LASALLE HOTEL

Phone: 3-3205

This is a copy of the front and back portions of the 1947 Blue Sox schedule. Perhaps the most interesting part of the schedule shows the involvement that the team had promoting and improving the recreational facilities in South Bend. They also supported a local girls baseball program for a number of seasons.

Bobby Sox League

Eastern Division

McKinley Chicks	9	1	.900
Marquette Red Wings	7	3	.700
Lincoln Fawns	6	4	.600
Leeper Lassies	4	6	.400
Studebaker Blue Sox	3	7	.300
Potawatomi Eagles	1	9	.100

Western Division

Bendix Belles	9	1	.900
Harrison Panthers	8	2	.800
Linden Comets	7	3	.700
Pulaski Falconettes	3	7	.300
Walkerfield Daisies	2	8	.200
Oliver Peaches	1	9	.100

In 1947, there were 12 teams in the local girls baseball league that was run through the South Bend Recreation Department. The program was supported by the profits made by the South Bend Blue Sox. At least eight of the twelve teams used nicknames that were used by All American Girls Professional Baseball League teams, including Blue Sox, Chicks, Red Wings, Lassies, Belles, Comets, Daisies and Peaches.

Blue Sox manager Chet Grant explains a situation to several players. At far right is Blue Sox outfielder Elizabeth Mahon.

The official Ticket Takers at Playland Park in 1947 for the Blue Sox. In the front, from left to right, are Mrs. Singleton, Mrs. Baeur, Hazel Meyers and Lillo Ewers. In the back row are Pearl Bauer, Mrs. Coil and Clifford Singleton.

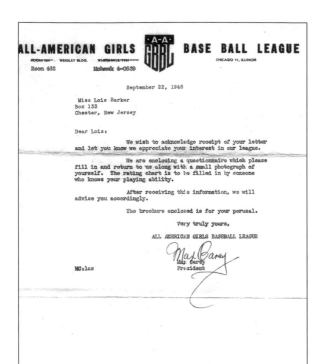

This letter was sent by All American Girls Professional Baseball League president Max Carey to Lois Barker of New Jersey, about playing in the league. Carey had played with the South Bend Central League baseball team in 1909 and 1910, before being sold to the Pittsburgh Pirates.

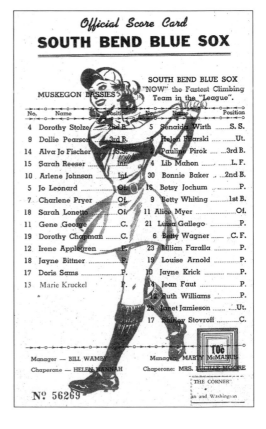

Here is one of the scorecards used by the Blue Sox in 1948. That season the Blue Sox and Racine Belles locked up in a 22-inning game on August 1. Blue Sox hurler Jean Faut pitched the whole game, bringing back to mind a 21-inning complete game pitched 38 years before by South Bend Central League pitcher John Henry Meyers.

Here is a 1951 scorecard cover from the Blue Sox. During the 1951 season, the Blue Sox won their first league championship.

This Blue Sox scorecard was used in the next to last season (1953). After the 1954 season, league directors voted to suspend play for 1955 and to try a comeback in 1956. It was a comeback that never happened.

1952

SCHEDULE

South Bend Blue Sox

World Champions

**AMERICAN GIRLS'
BASEBALL LEAGUE**
(Tenth Season)

Of all the schedules created for the Blue Sox, the more unique-looking is the one from 1952. A die-cut baseball design made it vastly different from the more traditional pocket schedules produced when the league was operated by a central organization.

Pictured is one of the final teams put on the field by the Blue Sox. In the front row, far left is Gertie Dunn, and in the back row, far right is manager Karl Winsch.

82

Former Blue Sox outfielder Elizabeth "Lib" Mahon is recognized in a ceremony in 1988 at a South Bend White Sox minor league game at Stanley Coveleski Regional Stadium. Making the presentation is South Bend Mayor Joe Kernan (middle) and South Bend White Sox General Manager John Baxter.

A total of eight former All American Girls Professional Baseball Leaguers were honored at Coveleski Stadium in 1988. Pictured from left to right are Lou Arnold, Janet "Pee Wee" Sears, Lillian Luckey, Elizabeth Mahon, Marie Kruckel, Betsy Jochum, Twi Shively and Nancy Rockwell.

All American Girls
Professional Baseball League

Golden Memories

REUNION

August 4 through 8, 1993

The Marriott
South Bend
Indiana

From August 4 through 8, 1993, it was a Turn-Back-The-Clock week in South Bend as the city was chosen to host a reunion commemorating the 50th anniversary of the All American Girls Professional Baseball League. Players, managers, umpires and fans all spent many hours reliving a unique time period for women and athletics.

This photograph was taken at the Marriott Hotel in South Bend near the end of the 50th anniversary celebration of the All American Girls Professional Baseball League. Pictured on the top are all the former All-Americans and their families and on the bottom are "Associate" members of the League's Player Association. The Association was created to perpetuate the memory of the players and the League for future generations.

PLAYERS

AAGPBL 50th REUNION 1993 SOUTH BEND, IN

ASSOCIATES

SEVEN

Seventh Inning

Personalities of the Game

Each community, no matter how large or how small, has individuals who stand out in many different capacities over the course of their history. In the history of South Bend baseball, it is no different. There are a number of individuals like that who will be profiled in this chapter. Now, of course, this is not the definitive list by any means. All of those individuals would need their own book!

There will be amateur and professionals; men and women; managers, players, a batboy and yes, even a dog! The three individuals who do not have an image to represent them will be talked about in this introduction; those with images will have their stories follow.

In the early to mid 1870s the first story takes place. The South Bend Clippers were one of the dominant teams in this area. One players who played for them on-and-off was Al Muchmore. It seemed that Muchmore was a bit of a free spirit. According to the newspaper reports of the day, both his hitting and fielding drew quite a bit of attention. When coming to bat, it was not unusual to see Muchmore toting three bats over his shoulder while puffing away on two cigars. His confidence at bat was such that as the pitcher went into his delivery, Muchmore would toss away two of the bats, but continue to puff away on his cigars!

In the field, he was just as colorful. He had two fielding tricks he liked to use. The first was to track down a fly ball as it was hit and then make the catch while prone on the ground. The other trick was that after he would catch a ball, he would throw it back to the infield and, in the same motion, turn a backward somersault and return to his position. Perhaps Ozzie Smith read about Muchmore and got his idea for some of his acrobatics from a South Bend Clipper of long ago!

The next story shows how sometimes even the National Pastime can "go to the dogs." On May 4, 1911, Elmer Moffitt of South Bend was on the mound against the Wheeling Stogies in a Central League game. After the first two batters went down, the third batter hit a bloop single into left. Normally that would be no cause for concern. However, as South bend left fielder Phil Geier went after the ball, a dog who had somehow gotten into the park, beat him to the ball and took off toward the foul line.

Geier then took off after the dog. Meanwhile, the Stogie hitter, who had been content with a bloop hit, suddenly found himself on a way to a three-bagger, courtesy of South Bend's tenth "man." Finally Geier caught the dog and got the ball back to the infied to hold the runner at third. Moffitt, who was a bit shaken from all the action on the last hit, then surrendered a base hit that knocked in the first run of the day. It was a run from which South Bend would never recover from as they dropped the game that day by a score of 4 to 3.

In 1914, the South Bend Southern Michigan League minor league club batboy was suspended by the owner. It seems that Leonard Smith, the team batboy, was very knowledgeable on the game of baseball. He had grown up with his father either playing, managing or serving as owner of a number of teams.

With his knowledge, he often times did not hesitate to tell players on his father's team when they erred. On one particular play, the comment and discussion became rather heated and ultimately led to his suspension from the team for 10 days!

Just a year before in Grand Rapids, Michigan, Smith, Sr. was part owner of that Central League team. During the season, young Leonard chose to take on an umpire when a close call went against the Grand Rapids team. The umpire ordered him off the field, but not before Leonard gave his opinion as to what he thought of Central League umpires. For that opinion, his father handed him a five-day suspension.

Needless to say, Leonard is probably the only batboy in professional baseball that was suspended in two different seasons, with two different teams and in two different leagues!

The South Bend Vernon Baseball team was managed by George Schmalzreid (middle row, second from left). Many times, he would take his turn as the starting pitcher on his team. Schmalzreid broke into baseball in 1898 with the Wyman Department Store team. He gained his fame as a pitcher, but what made his talent special is that he one had one arm. Perhaps his best game occurred when he was playing for the Goosepastures in 1899 when they were facing the Polish Turners. In that game Schmalzreid struck out 18 hitters, hit a two-run triple and, according to the newspaper, "all through the game picked out liners with his one hand."

A barber by trade, George Schmalzreid made a name for himself on the local baseball scene as "a one-armed twirler". Based on newspaper accounts, between 1899 and 1903, he compiled a record of 17-8. Perhaps the biggest handicap that he had to overcome was how the newspapers spelled his name. During his playing career, there were at least 12 variations (13 if you included the correct spelling) of his name in local box scores.

Frank Lichnerowicz was born in South Bend in 1892. He grew up playing sandlot baseball and became well known for his power. However, most people who saw him play would not recognize him by that name. The local baseball fans knew him as "Buck" Connors. Although he played mainly in the local industrial league with the team from Singers, he hit a number of home runs that are still talked about today. Especially so on July 26, 1927, when Connors belted a ball over the fence, across a major street and smack into the plate glass window of what was then, the Nowinski Bros. Meat Market. That shot was estimated to have traveled over 600 feet! His prolific power was still legendary years after he hung-up his spikes. Even his obituary on December 31, 1968, referred to him as the "Babe Ruth of South Bend."

Ben Piotrowski may have been one of the greatest pitchers in South Bend baseball history. "Big Ben," as he was known, compiled a record in high school of 29 wins against only two losses in a career that spanned from 1929 to 1931. That included 16 straight wins (1930–31) and 298 strikeouts in 186 innings pitched! Although he was signed by the Cleveland Indians, he never did advance out of the minors. Because of his great arm, he may have pitched too many innings too soon, hurting his arm. After a couple of seasons, his arm seemed to bounce back, but by then he would just play for a number of teams in South Bend until he retired.

Perhaps no other homegrown South Bend ballplayer had his career followed like "Ollie" Bejma. In 1926, Bejma got his start with the Studebaker Athletics team. His journey would then lead through a number of minor league season before finally hitting the major leagues with the St. Louis Browns in 1934. Many from the local Polish-American community traveled to Comiskey Park in Chicago on July 4 of that year to honor him with an "Ollie Bejma Day"! In 95 games with the Browns that year, Bejma hit .295 while playing shortstop, second, third base and the outfield. He played for the Browns from 1934-36 and then in 1939 he was with the Chicago White Sox. And while in the minor leagues in Minneapolis he was noticed by Charles Schultz, creator of the Peanuts comic strip. Schultz was a huge fan of the team and of Bejma and worked him into the strip!

A 45-year old catcher is generally not a sought after commodity in baseball. However, if that catch is Ted "Double Duty" Radcliffe, the team manger might just take that chance. That's what John "Lefty" Gunn of the Studebaker Local No. 5 baseball team did in 1948. Gunn signed Radcliffe (who would turn 46 in July) to a contract and was not disappointed. In 53 games, Radcliffe hit .292 and led the team with seven homers and 36 runs batted in. He also took several turns on the mound and compiled a 2.73 earned run average. This photograph of Radcliffe was taken at Coveleski Stadium in the summer of 1989. In the summer of 2004, at age 102, Radcliffe will be enshrined in the South Bend Baseball Hall of Fame!

From the 1930s to 1950s very few people were better known in the baseball circle than Roy Root. He got his start in the late 1930s as a player but is more remembered for his managing and promotion of local amateur and semi-pro baseball with the Hoosier Beers and later the South Bend Indians. For five consecutive seasons (1941–1945) his teams won the Northern Indiana League title. In this photograph, Root is pictured with some of his team hardware. Root

also brought in many Negro League teams to play his team or other Negro League clubs. His career record was 177-141 with 38 of those wins coming against the likes of Negro League teams such as the Kansas City Monarchs, Memphis Red Sox and Chicago American Giants. In 1994, the Michiana Over-Thirty Baseball League named their three divisions (Roy) Root, (Ted) Radcliffe and (Jean) Faut, honoring local baseball personalities.

In 1916, South Bend was back in the Central League, a minor league circuit, which they had originally entered in 1903. The home field, Springbrook Park, had not changed, but the names on the roster sure had. Among them was a 22 year old, right-handed pitcher named Alex "Red" McColl who was in his second year of pro baseball. During the 1916 season McColl would go 16-15 with a 2.30 earn run average for the South Bend club. He was also chosen as the top-fielding pitcher in the Central League that year.

Some 17 seasons after he had played with the South Bend Central League team, Alex "Red" McColl had his contract purchased by a major league team in 1933. At age 39, Alex was now a pitcher with the American League Washington Senators! In four games, he was 1-0 with an earned run average of 2.65 and, for good measure, he tossed two scoreless innings against the New York Giants in the World Series!

"Red" McColl (right) and John Kovach of the Northern Indiana Historical Society meet in South Bend in July of 1986—70 years after "Red" had been a pitcher for the local minor league team.

The greatest contact hitter to ever play professional baseball in South Bend was Josephine "Jo-Jo" D'Angelo. In 1943, the first year of the All American Girls Professional Baseball League, D'Angelo was patrolling centerfield for the Blue Sox. Playing in 104 games that season, she struck out only three times—or better stated, she fanned once for each 119.3 trips she made to the plate! She also stole 53 bases and led the league outfielders in assists with 22! That season, she was also a participant in the league All-Star game under the lights at Wrigley Field and got her teams' only hit of the night.

No professional pitcher ever dominated her opponent like South Bend Blue Sox right-hander Jean Faut. Playing with the local team in the All American Girls Professional Baseball League from 1946 to 1953, she was a force to be reckoned with. Three times (1949, 1950 and 1952) she won 20 or more games and narrowly missed a fourth time when she won "only" 19. In 1952, while going 20-2, her earned run average was 0.52. Faut hurled four no-hitters (1948, 1949, 1951 and 1953) and two of those were perfect games! For her career she finished with a record of 140-64 (.686) with an earned run average of 1.23. Faut retired from baseball after the 1953 season at age 28.

Many honors came late in life to Stanley Coveleski, including his induction to the National Baseball Hall of Fame in 1969 by a vote by the Committee on Veterans. In this photograph, Coveleski (at right) is holding a plaque from his induction into the National Polish-American Sports Hall of Fame. Seeing him honored so late in his life, his wife Frances offered her opinion on the subject of his 1969 induction. "If they (National Baseball Hall of Fame) would have called me about his selection after he (Coveleski) had died, I would have told them what they could have done with their award. If you can honor someone who's living so they can enjoy it, best not to do it at all."

Standing in front of the Heinz 57 box is Paul "Pop" Frankel who was bring honored for his, you guessed it, 57 years in local baseball during the 1951 season. That year, Frankel was managing the Miller-Anderson baseball team. To Pop's left in the light shirt and dark pants are his team sponsor, Dennis Miller. To the right of Frankel (handing him a bottle) is coach Bill Magley.

EIGHT

Eighth Inning

Lull in the Game

As in the case of many communities, there came a time when the once actives baseball programs seem to almost disappear. Of course, that was not really the case—youth programs, high school and American Legion teams were still numerous—but the major difference was the major downsizing of the adult baseball teams that once flourished.

In the late 1940s, the number of strong semi-pro and amateur baseball teams began to fade. In the early 1950s, the South Bend Indians of Roy Root who had been using Lippincott Park as their home base, had their park taken from underneath them by Studebakers who invoked a "reposition clause." With no place for them to play, the program faded away.

At the end of 1954, the South Bend Blue Sox of the All American Girls Professional Baseball League also played their last game as the league suspended play for 1955. They never resumed playing on a league basis.

There are a number of reasons these changes occurred. From a financial standpoint, it cost a lot of money operate a top-notch semi-pro baseball team. As the same factors affected other cities, competition dried-up and the games that could be found were farther and farther away from South Bend. To make it feasible to operate, the team would not only have to travel, but they would have to host visiting teams and guarantee them a certain amount of money to make the visit worthwhile.

Also, it terms of some of the larger companies who once sponsored these great team, some of the business were cutting back on expenses, cutting employees, and in some cases the companies closed-up permanently. That was the case for teams like Singers, Studebakers, Wilson Brothers and Oliver Chilled Plow to name just a few.

For the All-American League, finances were also an issue. During the last few years of the league, many teams drastically cut their budgets. There soon was no money for girls baseball programs and recruiting of new talent. Without being able to replace the players who were retiring, the player pool grew smaller and smaller.

And the advent of television in most homes after World War II, provided families the chance to have an additional form of entertainment that had previously not existed. That, coupled with the move from the city into the suburbs, created fewer ties of an earlier time when you worked, lived, shopped and played in your neighborhood.

While the 1950s and 1960s were the lull in terms of baseball in South Bend, it certainly was not the end—just a rest for the active years yet to come.

Players from the Central Catholic Baseball team await the beginning of the 1950 season.

Many of the high schools used hand drawn sketches at the beginning of yearbook or newspaper sections on various sports and activities. This sketch was used by Riley High School in 1951 to start space devoted to their baseball team.

This is the 1952 Singer-sponsored Pony League team. Front row players, from left to right, are Jerry Swartz, John Bejma, Freddie Kroll, Tommy Gruber and Ronnie Jagneski. In the back row are John Mirocha, Frank Sikorski, Carl Andrysiak, Eugene Dziubinski, Maike Boulanger and Paul Niezgodski. The team used Pulaski Park as their home field.

This is another of the Singer youth-sponsored teams. The team of nine to 11 year olds were coached by Joe Redling. Singers had once produced some of the best amateur and semi-pro baseball teams in South Bend and in its final years as a local company, sponsored a number of youth baseball teams in South Bend.

First-year South Bend LaSalle baseball coach Ben Hoevel hits to the infield prior to a game against Central High School in 1967. It was the first year of baseball for LaSalle.

Jim Ulrich takes a pitch for a ball during a game for Riley High School in the spring of 1957.

Lefthanded pitcher Dennis Parrish kicks and gets ready for a game for Jackson High School in 1967. That season, he had four wins and an earned run average of 2.88.

Perhaps one of the biggest jumpstarts to this era of baseball was the 1970 state baseball championship that was won by Clay High School. In this photograph, Clay pitcher Andy Replogle (No. 41) is visited by his manager Jim Reinbold (middle) during the final game.

Pitcher Bob Butsch of Adams High School fires a pitch during his sectional no-hitter against Jackson High School in 1971. That season, Butsch had two no-hit games; the other was against South Bend Washington.

NINE

Ninth Inning

For the Love of the Game

The lull experienced by South Bend baseball in the 1950s and 1960s slowly began to reverse itself. Youth programs, high school and American Legion teams had kept the interest going and now those players would get ready to pass along their love of the game to a new generation of baseball players, both male and female.

While in the 1960s there had been a handful of adult baseball teams playing in the area, that movement was stepped-up in 1975 with the creation of the Michiana Amateur Baseball League. On of the driving forces in that league was Gary Letherman, who had gotten his first taste of managing through the efforts of Paul "Pop" Frankel. He was joined by William "Pop" Sheridan, another manager, and Norris "Gadget" Ward who became the first commissioner for the league. Their efforts are still going strong today.

Beginning in the 1960s and taking off in the 1970s was the creation of the local Mexican-American League. At first, the league provided an opportunity for Hispanic baseball players and today, it is a melting pot of ethnicity.

As local players get older though, there was not a lot of opportunity for them to play baseball, especially since many of the leagues played on weekdays and weekends. Playing with and against college age players of those in their early 20s was difficult for the athlete who might be in their late 30s. Their only option to play ball was limited to slowpitch softball.

In 1992, the older players suddenly got a baseball reprieve. The Michiana Over-Thirty League began with the hopes of having enough players to have pick-up games once a week. In their first year of play, the league fielded four teams, three in South Bend and one in Elkhart, Indiana. Just two years later, the league exploded, carrying 12 teams, in three divisions named for local baseball legends: Roy Root, Ted "Double Duty" Radcliffe and Jean Faut.

As opportunities began to grow for the men, so was the case for women who wanted to play baseball. In 1996, between the efforts of USA Baseball, Inc. and the American Amateur Baseball Congress (AABC) a new women's baseball league formed. An amateur organization, the Great Lakes Women's Baseball League was the first interstate baseball league for women since the All American League had folded in 1954. That first year, there were five teams in 1996: South Bend Belles, Chicago Blue Notes, Fort Wayne Phantoms, Battle Creek Stars and Lansing Stars. It was interesting to note that South Bend, Chicago, Fort Wayne and Battle Creek all formerly had franchises in the All American League.

Of the five original teams, South Bend is the only one still active in the Great Lakes League as the 2004 season gets ready to open. The South Bend team (who changed their nickname to Blue Sox in 1999) have also been active in creating a girls baseball program, following in the footsteps of their predecessors in the All American Girls Professional Baseball League.

If that were not enough to satisfy the local baseball fans and players, South Bend again became the home of a minor league baseball team. In 1985, efforts started on bringing a minor league baseball team to South Bend. One of the first things to be looked at were what type of team would be available and what were the local playing facilities like.

The Class A Midwest League was soon getting ready to expand and so an opportunity was there. In order to have the team though, it was decided that the local facilities were not very impressive for professional baseball, even for ball on the Class A level.

The City of South Bend secured financing for a brand new facility that was to be constructed in downtown. The 5,200-seat facility would be called Stanley Coveleski Regional Stadium and in 1988, for the first time in over 55 years, minor league baseball was played. The local team is entering its seventeenth season of play. The first nine seasons, the club was affiliated with the Chicago White Sox and for the last eight years, the Arizona Diamondbacks have been the major league affiliation. From 1988 to 1993, the teams name reflected their major league affiliation and they were known as the South Bend White Sox. In 1994, a local flavor was given to the team as a new nickname was selected. That season, the team became known as the South Bend SilverHawks. A Silverhawk was a type of car once produced by the Studebaker Corporation in South Bend.

In the early 1970s, one of the most dominating high school players was Dave Wood of Washington. Not only was he an outstand hurler, but he also held down first base when he wasn't pitching and carried a lethal bat at the plate. After high school, Wood spent some time in the Chicago Cub farm system.

Perhaps no high school team in the early 1970s had a better 1-2 mound punch than Dave Wood and Joel Finch (No. 14) pictured here. The two would alternate between the mound and first base and kept Washington as one of the dominant teams during their high school days. After his high school days, Finch was drafted by and briefly played with the Boston Red Sox in the American League.

Pitching can be a hazardous occupation! In this photograph, pitcher John Kovach of the South Bend Yankees gets upended by Rich Kennedy of the LaPorte Sportsmen while covering the plate in a Michiana Amateur Baseball League game. In the background to the right is Dan Rooks and to the left is Dave Petersen, Kovach's Yankee teammates.

It is June of 1987. The finishing touches are being put on Stanley Coveleski Regional Stadium. The 5,200-seat stadium would open for business in the summer of 1987 and in 1988, it became the home to South Bend's Class A Midwest League team.

Here is an aerial view of Coveleski Stadium on April 10, 1988. A near capacity crowd saw professional baseball return to South Bend in a winning fashion. That day, the South Bend White Sox defeated the Peoria Chiefs by a score of 2 to 1 on a home run by Mike Maksudian. Winning pitcher that day was Curt Hasler, who hurled a three-hitter.

Mike "The Sheik" Maksudian ushered in a new era of professional baseball in South Bend when he belted a game winning home run on opening day. He remained a fan favorite throughout that season!

One of the first members of the new minor league field staff that was signed was longtime South Bend baseball coach Jim Reinbold. Best know as the head coach at Clay High School, his team won a state title in 1970.

South Bend White Sox firstbase coach grimaces at a call. Through the White Sox era and into the SilverHawk name and later franchise change, Reinbold was the one constant found in the coaching box. In 2000, he was inducted into the South Bend Baseball Hall of Fame.

Since it's first minor league season, one of the fan favorites in entertainment is an appearance by the Famous Chicken. For a number of years, he would often appear twice during the season because of his popularity! Here, the Famous Chicken tries his hand in the coaches' box at Coveleski Stadium.

Pictured is a typical summer evening at Coveleski Stadium in South Bend. This view is from the pressbox looking out toward centerfield.

Manager Rick Patterson took the helm of the South Bend White Sox in 1989. His club caught fire early and never looked back. The team record of 44-18 in the first half of the season and 44-18 in the second half propelled them into the Midwest League playoffs. Five straight wins later and the South Bend White Sox were the Midwest League champions! It was South Bend's first minor league crown since 1910. Patterson also managed South Bend in 1990 and compiled a mark of 77-57. In the summer of 2003, he was inducted into the South Bend Baseball Hall of Fame.

A key figure on the 1989 South Bend White Sox was closer Scott Radinsky. A lefty, Radinsky would amass 31 saves for the South Bend club during that championship season. In the spring of 1990, Radinsky made the jump from Class A to the major leagues with the Chicago White Sox.

In 1990, Scott Cepicky became the first South Bend baseball player in over 45 years to win a batting title. That season, hitting .312. Betsy Jochum of the South Bend Blue Sox had last won a South Bend batting title by hitting .296 to lead all hitters in the All American Girls Professional Baseball League.

One of the best pitchers on the South Bend White Sox staff in 1990 was Sam Chavez. On a pace during the season to win 25 games or more in the Midwest League, Chavez moved-up to the next level after winning his 15th game.

During the winter an idea was hatched to create a league for South Bend baseball players to again play the game they grew up with. Bruce Klimek (in background) and John Kovach (foreground) introduced the league in 1992 and were able to field a four team league. In two years, the team totals had jumped to a total of 12 clubs. In this photograph, Klimek and Kovach are with the Dugout Ancient Mariners.

In the spring of 1994, Indiana University South Bend was fielding their first baseball team, coached by Ron Compton. Pictured is 35-year old knuckleball pitcher John Kovach, who made it through two cuts to make the team comprised of players age 18-22. In 16 pitching appearances, Kovach had an earned run average of 3.12 and surrendered only one walk in 38 innings pitched.

When the Diamonbacks chose South Bend as one of their farm clubs, they did so with open arms. No less than twice in the brief time of their affiliation have they brought the major league team to South Bend for an exhibition game. In this photograph, Diamondback manager Bob Brenley shakes the hand of Dick Schofield, South Bend SilverHawks manager before the August 2002 exhibition. (Photo Courtesy of Brent Miller.)

Andrew McCreery, South Bend SilverHawks first baseman, awaits a pickoff throw to nail a runner from the Battle Creek Yankees who has wandered too far off base. (Photo Courtesy of Brent Miller.)

Jeff Cook is a popular player for the SilverHawks because of his hard-nosed play. Cook joined South Bend in 2003 and hit .279 and stole 10 bases in 12 attempts. He has returned to South Bend for the 2004 season. (Photo Courtesy of Brent Miller.)

Pitcher Chad Scarberry kicks his leg on his delivery to the plate during a game at Coveleski Stadium. The 2004 season is his first in South Bend. In 2003, Scarberry pitched for the Class A Yakima (WA) ball club.

Outfielder John Kaplan takes a tight inside pitch during a 2004 game at Coveleski Stadium.

In 1996, women's baseball returned to South Bend as the five-team Great Lakes Womens Baseball League (an amateur circuit) was established. South Bend pitcher Joy Kroemer of the Belles throws a pitch at Oldsmobile Park in Lansing, Michigan. In 1997, Kroemer played for the Colorado Silver Bullets, professional women's baseball team and in 1998, she played for the Buffalo NightHawks of the Ladies Professional Baseball League.

By 1999, the South Bend had changed their nickname to the "Blue Sox," echoing the heritage of the old All American Girls Professional Baseball League team. Mel Carter, pictured here, works off the mound in a game at Coveleski Stadium. In 1999, cater was selected as a National MVP for her play in centerfield and on the mound.

Pitcher Laura Patterson is one of only two South Bend pitchers to go undefeated in a season on the mound. In 1996, Patterson went 2-0 and picked up both of her wins in a doubleheader, In game one, she was the winner as a starter and in game two, she picked-up the win in relief.

Jessica Higgins joined the Belles in 1997 as a 16-year-old first baseman. That first season, she hit over .300 and averaged a run batted in for every hit to her credit. Higgins also went three-for-three in an exhibition game that same season against a men's over-30 baseball team. To the right of Higgins is Carol Sheldon of the Lansing (MI) Stars.

Jill Kleiser of the Blue Sox delivers a pitch during the Great Lakes Women's Baseball Tournament at Coveleski Stadium. The tourney, which began in 1997, is the longest running North American women's baseball tourney and will be in its ninth season in 2004.

In 2000, the Blue Sox honored its two long-time umpires (Burl Swain and Jack Kennedy) with a special plaque. Pictured from left to right are: Chris Spychalski, Swain, Kennedy and Laura Patterson. Spychalski and Patterson were original members of the South Bend team in 1996.

South Bend Blue Sox batgirl Emily Kovach participates in a girls baseball clinic at Tiger Stadium in Chicago.

During the course of their existence, the Blue Sox have traveled all over North American for tournaments. In this photograph, Blue Sox manager John Kovach and his daughter Emily pose for a picture while the team was participating in an invitational tournament in Toronto, Canada, in 2001.

Melissanne Miller played thirdbase and pitched for the Blue Sox in 2001. That same year, she was chosen to play in the first-ever, Women's Baseball World Series in Toronto, Canada.

Mayoral Assistant Freddie Thon presents certificates of recognition to some of the members of Team USA who won the first Women's World Series by defeating Japan in Toronto in 2001. pictured from left to right are Thon, Melissanne Miller, Joni Stegeman and Allie Adams.

In 2004, Katie Pappa became the youngest National MVP in women's baseball history. At age 14, in her second season as a member of the Blue Sox, Pappa led her team in batting average, hits doubles and runs batted in. In this photograph she readies herself to deliver a pitch.

Katie Pappa strokes a double during the 2004 Citrus Blast opening season baseball tourney in Ft. Myers, Florida. Hitting .500 in that tourney led her on her way to a National MVP Award at the season's end.

South Bend Blue Sox manager John Kovach (No. 1) and hitter Katie Pappa (No. 12) engage in a discussion with umpire Jack Kennedy.

Blue Sox pitcher Jerrika Christianson is in mid-leg kick during a pitching appearance in the Citrus Blast Tournament. Christianson fanned seven batters in her three innings of work in that game.

Umpire Tom Giffen talks to pitcher Blue Sox pitcher Jerrika Christianson during a player change during the 2004 Citrus Blast Tournament.

Shanon Singleton grew up playing baseball. In 1996, she again got the chance to play as a member of the South Bend Belles. An accomplished pitcher and hitter, she has come the closest to a no-hitter than any other South Bend pitcher. In 1996, she fired a one-hitter versus the Fort Wayne Phantoms. In 2002, she was voted as a National MVP for her outstanding season on the mound and at the plate. Here, Singleton fires a pitch while on the mound at Coveleski Stadium.

Since 1999, Andi Ermis has been a solid performer with the Blue Sox. Several seasons have found her hitting .300 or better. A catcher-outfielder, Ermis is one of the fastest players in the Great Lakes League. In 2003, she was named a National MVP as she set career high marks in batting, runs scored and stolen bases.

Every baseball player loves an opportunity to meet a professional player. In this photograph, Ila Borders (left) poses with Ashley Holderman of the Blue Sox during a baseball clinic at the Skydome in Toronto Canada in 2000. Borders had pitched for the St. Paul Saints, an independent pro baseball team in the Northern League. Holderman has been a member of the South Bend team since 1997. A pitcher and first baseman, she holds all the team defensive records at first base and tops the team career-wise in games and innings pitched.

Lefty Ashley Holderman stares down for her sign. In 2000, she led the team in games, innings pitched and wins while hitting over .400! After the season, she was voted as a National MVP.

Lori Bryant gets ready to fire a pitch while throwing in relief during a Great Lakes Invitational Tournament game. Bryant is also an outstanding catcher and has one of the best throwing arms in the Great Lakes League. Not a superstitious person, Bryant has worn number 13 her entire career with South Bend, dating back to 1996.

It's conference time at the mound. Pictured from left to right are Katie Pappa, Ashley Nicolls, Amy Schneider and Shanon Singleton discussing some defensive strategy during a game at the 2003 Citrus Blast.

South Bend Blue Sox catcher Nicolette Franck blocks a Florida Crush player from the plate during game action at the 2003 Citrus Blast.

Nicolette Franck shows the ball to the umpire after her block of the plate and tag of a Florida Crush runner.

South Bend Blue Sox catcher Robin Wallace reaches for a pitch during the 2002 Great Lakes Invitational. Wallace assumed the role that weekend of player-manager of the Blue Sox and led them to a second place finish in the tourney.

Ericka Johnson, a fourteen year-old outfielder with the Blue Sox in 2003, looks down to third for a sign from her coach. Johnson finished the 2003 season hitting an even .300.